sydney
& beyond

Steve Parish

PUBLISHING

Previous pages: Sydney Opera House and Sydney Harbour Bridge at dusk.　　*Above:* Relaxing on Coogee Beach, Sydney.　　*Following pages:* A view across the Gap to Watsons Bay, Sydney Harbour and the city.

Introduction

New South Wales is a State of enormous visual variety, in natural and created landscapes, in vegetation and in wildlife. Even within one location, there are many visual time-levels. For example, looking at the Three Sisters, in the scenic Blue Mountains, it is possible to see 200 million years of geological history, written in layer upon layer of warm-coloured sandstone. The stately formations bring to mind the more recent Aboriginal legend of their Dreamtime creation, a story which may be many thousands of years old. The sheer walls of Kanangra represent the cliffs which two centuries ago hampered the attempts of early European settlers to cross these magnificent mountains. The cable car suspended high above the Jamison Valley, and the jaunty little train which carries visitors to the valley floor and back again, symbolise modern methods of obtaining views of natural beauty which previously could be seen only by birds or human daredevils.

Just over 1300 people of mainly British origins settled at Sydney Cove in 1788. Since then, much of New South Wales has been changed by clearing, by mining, by the pastoral and agricultural industries and by industrialisation. Enormous areas of untouched natural beauty still remain, and there are many fascinating towns and historic places. When putting together this book I found it very difficult to decide what to include. Some images selected themselves – Sydney Harbour, a paddlewheeler on the Murray, the Australian Alps in winter, and Jenolan Caves are examples. Others seemed required to complete a story, or were just too appealing to leave out. But in the end there were many great pictures of great places which simply could not be included.

I hope you enjoy the images chosen to celebrate this wonderful State.

Steve Parish

Sydney – a great city

Sydney stands in magnificent natural surroundings. It stretches from the shores of lovely Sydney Harbour and the sparkling Tasman Sea westwards towards the spectacular Blue Mountains. To the south lies Royal National Park and northwards the seaside holiday resorts of the Central Coast of New South Wales.

Four million people live in Sydney, an exciting, energetic business capital that offers sophisticated entertainment, fine restaurants, excellent hotels and world-class shopping. However, this first of Australia's cities is proud of its origins and makes the most of its national character and its unique setting. Sydney Harbour, the Harbour Bridge and Opera House, Darling Harbour, the Sydney Tower, the Queen Victoria Building, the Town Hall, The Rocks, Circular Quay, the Botanic Gardens, galleries, museums, beaches such as Manly, Bondi and Coogee – with these and many more attractions, Sydney is one of the world's great cities.

Left: Sydney's lovely setting on the shores of the Harbour is portrayed from Point Piper, past the City, the Opera House and the Harbour Bridge.
Following pages 6 & 7: View of Sydney Harbour – the Opera House is on the left, Circular Quay and the city are in the centre, and the Harbour Bridge is on the right.
Pages 8 & 9: From North Sydney over the City, showing Luna Park, the Harbour Bridge, the Royal Botanic Gardens, the Opera House and Darling Harbour.
Pages 10 & 11: Weekend yacht racing on Sydney Harbour.

Dawn breaking over the Sydney Opera House and City, seen from Cremorne Point.

Following pages: Sydney Harbour Bridge crosses the Harbour in one massive span, dominating the waterfront.

13

Above: The old Manly Ferry the *South Steyne* is permanently moored at Darling Harbour.

Darling Harbour

Sydney's Darling Harbour is close to the city centre and can be reached by water, by road, by monorail or on foot. The Harbourside complex occupies 54 hectares and offers around that number of waterfront restaurants and cafes, shopping in the Festival Marketplace, and displays in the Convention and Exhibition Centre. The Powerhouse Museum nearby is full of fascinating exhibits, the Australian Maritime Museum offers nautical history and the Sydney Aquarium houses a variety of Australia's marine and freshwater creatures. Between the complex and city is the beautiful Chinese Garden.

Opposite: Looking across Darling Harbour to the Harbourside complex.

Sydney's beaches

Within easy reach of Sydney are about 30 wonderful beaches, with picturesque rocky headlands guarding stretches of sand washed by the blue waters of the Tasman Sea. Many of these beaches have great surf, all share a relaxed atmosphere, and for those who do not wish to swim or sunbake, there are plenty of seaside walks, and places to eat, shop and play games. In summer, there are Surf Lifesaving Carnivals, which provide excitement and entertainment. The Surf Lifesaving movement, which began on Sydney beaches in the early 1900s, has saved countless distressed swimmers and has provided a model for similar services world wide.

Bondi, south of the entrance to Sydney Harbour and only half an hour by road from the city centre, is internationally famous for its golden sand, its surf and its boulevard. South of Bondi are Coogee, Maroubra, the sheltered beaches of Botany Bay and the delights of North Cronulla and Cronulla.

Manly, just north of North Head at the entrance to the Harbour, has both harbour and ocean beaches. The list of magnificent beaches north of Manly includes Dee Why, Narrabeen, Newport, Whale and Palm.

Right: Looking over Bondi to more southerly beaches.
Following pages: A lazy day at Manly Beach.
Pages 22 & 23: A view west to North Harbour over Manly Beach.

North from Sydney

The 30 kilometre stretch of coastline between Sydney and Palm Beach, the famed "Northern Beaches" area, is known for its surf and is home to over 20 surf lifesaving clubs. For those who wish for a quiet time by the seaside, there are plenty of tidal pools and secluded stretches of sand. At Narrabeen, the saltwater Narrabeen Lakes have formed behind the beach, and are popular for sailing, canoeing and windsurfing. The final splendid beach of the series, Palm Beach, leads to Barrenjoey Head, whose dramatic bulk is crowned by a stately lighthouse.

Inland, Ku-ring-gai Chase National Park, with its forests, sandstone rock formations and abundant wildlife, attracts bushwalkers and nature lovers.

Left: Palm Beach leads to Barrenjoey Light. On the right, the protected, calm bay called Pittwater.
Following pages: Getting away from it all, on a Central Coast beach, north of Sydney.

The Central Coast

The Central Coast of New South Wales was first settled in 1839 and the hinterland between the Great Dividing Range and the Pacific Ocean is full of small, fertile farms. Since the railway connected the area with Sydney in 1889, the Central Coast has formed a holiday playground for the city.

Today, the Pacific Highway runs through spectacular sandstone country, across the scenic Hawkesbury River and through the 12 000 hectare Brisbane Water National Park and Gosford. Nearby, Brisbane Water and Tuggerah Lake form two sides of a peninsula rich in waterways and beauty spots. Further inland, Yengo and Dharug National Parks offer rugged wilderness areas of rainforest and eucalypt woodland to challenge adventurers.

Left: Looking over the town of Gosford to Brisbane Water and Brisbane Water National Park.
Following pages: Terrigal, 12 kilometres from Gosford, is a popular beach resort on the Central Coast.

Relaxing at the beach

Above: Fun in the sun on Avoca Beach.

Opposite: A glorious day at Terrigal Beach.

The further north you go along the New South Wales coast, the sooner the sea warms up after winter's chill. Come summer and the sand is colourful with beach towels, bright hats and umbrellas. If the surf is quiet, there's beach volleyball or a game of cricket to keep the energetic happy, while many beach-goers are happy just to read a book, or dunk themselves in the shallows, or stroll along the tide line admiring the sights of the sea and its devotees.

Rainforest magic

Above: A scene full of magic in Barrington Tops National Park.

After providing water for the vineyards, dairies, farms and towns of the Hunter Valley, the Hunter and Manning Rivers finally run to the sea on New South Wales' Central Coast. They have their sources in the high basalt plateaus of the Barrington and Gloucester Tops, west of Newcastle, where Barrington Tops National Park protects a remarkable variety of plant life. Above the snowline are Snow Gums and subalpine grassland, while lower down in sheltered valleys are stands of subtropical rainforest and even groves of ancient Antarctic Beech trees. This is World Heritage listed forest.

Opposite: Williams River, Barrington Tops National Park.
Preceding pages: Somersby Falls, Brisbane Water National Park.

Port Stephens

North of Newcastle are some of Australia's loveliest east coast beaches, which provide the busy centre of industry with a choice of playgrounds.

Port Stephens, with its picturesque waterways and wonderful surf beaches, is typical of these Central Coast Pacific paradises. It was sighted by Captain Cook in 1770 and today its tranquillity testifies to the fact that in this town there have always been far-sighted citizens to oppose unwise industrial development. Fishing is a major pursuit here and a Game Fishing Festival is held each February.

Fishing on Nelsons Bay, Port Stephens.

The North Coast

New South Wales' northern coastline has a unique climate, warm, moist and pleasant all the year round. The Great Dividing Range runs close to the coast, and its slopes and the flood plains of the rivers which run from mountains to sea were once covered by magnificent forests. Today, much of the tall timber has been harvested and bananas and other subtropical crops abound. However, the wild areas which remain, with their rainforests, rugged gullies, rushing waterways and tumbling waterfalls, are breathtaking and 16 of them have been combined to form a World Heritage area.

The coastline itself is a constant revelation of scenic attractions, with sweeping beaches, picturesque headlands, sheltered, sandy coves and charming towns. The Northern Coast offers adventurous experiences, such as sailing, scuba diving, game-fishing, white water rafting and bushwalking. Just as satisfying for many are the exploration of galleries, craft shops and historic sites, or pursuing the gastronomic delights of this marvellous coastal area.

A peaceful scene in the Northern Rivers area of New South Wales.

Port Macquarie

A Port Macquarie beach and headland.

In a favoured setting at the mouth of the Hastings River, Port Macquarie is one of the most popular holiday spots on the New South Wales coast. Sugar cane is grown on the fertile plains near the port, timber-getting is a traditional occupation, fishing and oyster-farming are important, but this enterprising town also offers various tourist-oriented attractions, including theme parks and nature parks.

Coffs Harbour

Above: Fishing vessels and pleasure craft at their marina in Coffs Harbour.

Following pages: The Dorrigo Hotel and War Memorial, Dorrigo.

During the 1860s and 70s, Coffs Harbour shipped out loads of prized Red Cedar logs from the forests nearby. Today, it is a fast-growing tourist city from which to explore superb beaches or to venture into nearby Dorrigo National Park. The harbour provides mooring for fishing and pleasure craft; in June and September, Humpback Whales may be seen offshore, travelling to and from their breeding grounds.

National parks of the northern mountains

The Great Dividing Range runs down coastal New South Wales from the Queensland to the Victorian border. In its northern reaches, it contains a number of national parks which showcase rugged mountain scenery and unique forests.

Dorrigo National Park protects what remains of the once-famous Dorrigo Scrub (the old name for rainforest). This is an area of misty mountains, great buttressed rainforest trees, orchids, ferns and wildlife.

Further inland lie Guy Fawkes River National Park, an area of breathtaking wilderness, and New England National Park, which offers temperate rainforest, Snow Gum woodland and the spectacular gorge carved by the Bellinger River in the rim of an ancient, extinct volcano.

Preceding pages: Dorrigo Falls, Dorrigo National Park.
Right: Crystal Shower Falls, along Wonga Walk, Dorrigo National Park.

Snow Gum woodland in New England National Park.

Ebor Falls in Guy Fawkes River National Park.

National parks of the North Coast

Yuraygir National Park stretches along the coast east of Grafton, in the Northern Rivers area of New South Wales.

The national parks of northern New South Wales are noted for their coastal scenery. Yuraygir National Park, in the Northern Rivers area, is in three sections which, between them, cover 60 kilometres of coast from Red Rock's jasper outcrop in the south to the Wooloweyah Estuary to the north. The park encloses the resorts of Wooli, Brooms Head and Minnie, and walking tracks give access to secluded beaches.

Crowdy Bay National Park, between Taree and Port Macquarie, is noted for its spring wildflowers and features rugged headlands, coastal dunes, lakes and heathlands.

Crowdy Head is a scenic feature of Crowdy Bay National Park, famous for its springtime wildflowers.

Above: The Cape Byron light can be seen for over 40 kilometres out to sea at night.
Opposite: Cape Byron is the most easterly point on the Australian mainland.

Byron Bay

The wonderful climate and unspoiled beaches of Byron Bay have made it a mecca for holiday-makers and for those who wish to live in idyllic surroundings. Once it was a timber-getting town, which diversified into dairying as soon as refrigeration made transporting produce from the green countryside to the distant cities practical. Today it is one of Australia's most notable beauty spots, which retains its small town atmosphere while catering to a growing number of enthusiastic visitors. Off shore, cool temperate waters from the southern coastline mingle with warmer tropical seas, creating a unique and fascinating marine world.

Mt Warning

Above: The distant silhouette of Mt Warning, seen over the town of Murwillumbah.

More than 20 million years ago, a gigantic volcano belched molten rock over 4000 square kilometres of the area which is now north-eastern New South Wales. When, after three million years, the volcano became inactive, the softer rocks of its central cone were worn away by weather: today its lava core stands as Mt Warning, west of Murwillumbah.

The tip of Mt Warning rises more than 1100 metres above sea level, and is the first place on Australia's east coast to catch the rays of the sun at dawn. The rainforested slopes of the mountain are included in Mt Warning National Park, while its rim is part of the Border Ranges National Park to the west, and of the Nightcap National Park to the south.

Opposite: Mt Warning, the core of a long-extinct volcano.

Lord Howe Island

Lord Howe Island was formed by volcanic activity which, around 80 million years ago, pushed part of the sea bed above the surface of the ocean. Today, this jewel of a subtropical island stands in the Tasman Sea some 500 kilometres due east of Port Macquarie, around two hours flying time from either Brisbane or Sydney. With its sandy, palm-fringed white beaches, turquoise lagoons, coral reefs and towering peaks. Lord Howe is everyone's ideal of an island paradise.

The group which consists of Lord Howe, the precipitous Balls Pyramid 2 kilometres to the south-east and the Admiralty Islands, became a World Heritage Area in 1982, is a national park and is administered by a Board responsible to the NSW Minister for Lands. The tranquillity of Lord Howe is guaranteed by limiting the number of visitors who may stay at any one time, and walking, birdwatching, fishing, reef-exploring and diving are popular recreations.

Left: Looking from North Ridge across the lagoon to Mts Lidgbird and Gower, Lord Howe Island.
Previous Pages: Oxley Wild Rivers National Park is a series of parks near Walcha, containing the watercourses which eventually make up the Macleay River.

Heading south from Sydney

From Sydney, excellent roads run south towards the Victorian border.

The Princes Highway skirts the western boundary of the Royal National Park, joins the Southern Freeway for a while, then takes the coastal route to Wollongong, Kiama and Nowra.

The Hume Highway is for a time transformed into the South Western Freeway, and eventually passes through picturesque Mittagong, Bowral, Moss Vale and Goulburn.

Whichever route is chosen, the pleasure in travelling these highways is watching the changing scene of the magnificent countryside as it sweeps past.

Driving south of Sydney on Princes Highway brings many coastal views such as this one near Kiama, south of Lake Illawarra.

Wollongong and Kiama

Above: Blow-hole Point and lighthouse, Kiama.　　*Opposite:* The coast road to Wollongong, near Clifton and Scarborough.

Wollongong, 80 kilometres south of Sydney, was once a port for timber, then coal: today, industrial shipping frequents nearby Port Kembla and Wollongong's harbour is home to pleasure and fishing craft. Inland, in valleys of the Illawarra escarpment, are rainforest remnants known for wildlife.

Thirty kilometres south of Wollongong is Kiama, a delightful holiday resort. Here, on a rocky point, the sea has created a famous blow-hole which can jet spray metres above the rocks. In the past, Kiama exported timber, as well as blue metal, which was used to pave Sydney's streets.

Following pages: Flagstaff Point, lighthouse and harbour, Wollongong.

The glorious South Coast

Above: Merimbula, once a port for diggers heading to the Snowy Mountains goldfields.

Jervis Bay, just south of Nowra, is noted for majestic coastal scenery and for the variety and content of its underwater habitats: it is one of Australia's most remarkable diving locations. The road heading south passes through towns such as Ulladulla, Batemans Bay, Narooma and Bermagui, the last two famous for big-game and recreational fishing.

Merimbula, at the northern end of Ben Boyd National Park, is a popular place for water sports of all kinds. Its other attractions include local rock oysters and a fine aquarium.

Opposite: Point Perpendicular and its lighthouse guard the entrance to Jervis Bay.

Eden

Above: The Eden fishing fleet at home in Twofold Bay.

The story of the Killers of Eden sounds like romance, but is fact. Whaleboats set out from the South Coast port of Eden as early as 1828, pursuing female Southern Right Whales which came into the sheltered coastline to calve. By 1840, lack of prey had switched the hunters' attention to Sperm Whales. A school of Killer Whales is reported to have assisted the whalers, herding their larger relatives into Twofold Bay so they could be harpooned. Whaling ceased many years ago, and today, Eden is a major fishing port. Whales still cruise past, but they are protected and a major tourist attraction.

Opposite: Fishing vessels at Eden, sunrise.

Morton and Budderoo National Parks

Morton National Park protects more than 154 000 hectares of rugged country, stretching from west of Kiama south down the Great Dividing Range. Budderoo National Park covers just 5700 hectares, east of the northern tip of Morton National Park.

These national parks contain wild areas, where the massive sandstone masses of the southern part of the Sydney Basin have been carved into ravines by the waters of the Shoalhaven, Clyde and Kangaroo Rivers. Eucalypt forests grow on the sandstone tops, and temperate rainforests flourish in the gorges. Swamps and catchments on the tops become streams which plunge over sandstone ledges to form falls such as Fitzroy, Belmore and Carrington. From July to December, the park heaths are bright with wildflowers.

Left: Belmore Falls, Morton National Park.
Following pages: Fitzroy Falls, Morton National Park; Carrington Falls, Budderoo National Park.

73

Kangaroo Valley

Above: Hampden Suspension Bridge was built across the Kangaroo River in 1898.

Twenty-three kilometres from Nowra, beautiful Kangaroo Valley lies along the escarpment of the Great Dividing Range which is included in Morton National Park. The New South Wales National Trust has classified the entire valley as worthy of classification. Known as Kangaroo Ground when settled in the early 1820s, Kangaroo Valley today is noted for its fertile fields and green pastures, a Pioneer Settlement Museum, craft shops, restaurants, and a country Music Festival held each October. Hampden Suspension Bridge was opened in 1898; only five days later, the old wooden bridge it replaced was unexpectedly removed by a flash flood.

Opposite: Kangaroo Valley, seen from Hindmarsh Lookout.

Above: Smiggins Hole was once a cattle camp but today is part of the large Perisher/Smiggins resort.

Above: Blue Cow Mountain is home to Blue Cow Guthega ski resort, reached by a railway called the Skitube.

Above: Charlottes Pass is named after Charlotte Adams, the first European woman to climb Mt Kosciusko.

The Australian Alps

In summertime, the high country of the Australian Alps is ablaze with snow daisies, billy buttons and other wildflowers. Bushwalkers trek its trails, climbers assault its rock faces, nature lovers stalk birds and other wildlife, binoculars at the ready, and every lake and stream has its rod and reel enthusiasts.

Come winter and a crystalline white blanket of snow covers the mountains. Nature might be sleeping until springtime arrives again, but the skiers who flock to the Alps cover the slopes with colour and activity.

Opposite: A winterbound Snow Gum.
Following pages: The Australian Alps from the air.

The Murray River

Above: River Red Gums line a backwater of the Murray in Moira State Forest.

Opposite: A paddlewheeler on the Murray near Mildura.

The mighty Murray rises in the Great Dividing Range, then flows for more than 2500 kilometres before entering the Southern Ocean. For much of its length, it forms the boundary between New South Wales and Victoria, supplying water for irrigation to both States. For much of the nineteenth century, the Murray was a busy commercial waterway. Today, paddlewheelers from towns on the Murray carry passengers who have come to enjoy the beauty of the great river.

Albury at dusk.

Albury

Morning mists on Lake Hume.

On the northern bank of the Murray River, Albury is part of the complex of Albury–Wodonga, twin cities which form a commercial and industrial centre for the Riverina district. Albury was settled in 1838, became a major paddlewheeler port, built its first riverboat in 1858 and in 1883 became the rail changeover depot, where New South Wales' train tracks meshed with Victoria's rail system, which used a different gauge track. Modern Albury treasures its history and has many protected buildings. It has fine theatre facilities, a museum and art galleries, and is a holiday centre which takes full advantage of the majestic Murray and nearby Lake Hume.

Heading west from Sydney

Above: A waterfall tumbles from a sandstone plateau, Kanangra Boyd National Park.

Today, it takes around 90 minutes to travel in a motor vehicle along the Great Western Highway from Sydney into the heart of the Blue Mountains. However, it took 25 years from the first European settlement at Sydney Cove for explorers to find a route over these rugged sandstone ranges. Early adventurers were baffled by valleys which led to sheer cliffs. In May 1813 Gregory Blaxland, William Lawson and William Charles Wentworth followed the ridge tops rather than the gullies, struggling through dense forest for nearly three weeks before sighting the plains on the further side of the mountains.

Opposite: Sheer cliffs like these in Kanangra Boyd National Park formed a barrier to early European exploration west of Sydney.

The Blue Mountains

The soft, hazy blue hues typical of the Blue Mountains are caused by the sun's rays making contact with the fine droplets of oil which rise into the air from the eucalypt trees of the area's forests. For many Australians, and an increasing number of visitors from all around the world, the Blue Mountains mean magical experiences of towering golden cliffs, sparkling waterfalls, mysterious forests and other wild places full of wildlife and sometimes unique plants.

The Blue Mountains contain 24 townships, the best known of which is Katoomba, which stands amidst a number of the Blue Mountains' most notable attractions.

Left: Katoomba, residential centre of the Blue Mountains, overlooks the Kedumba Valley. The Three Sisters, the Giant Stairway, the Scenic Railway, Echo Point and Katoomba Falls are nearby attractions.
Following pages: The Three Sisters, sandstone pillars which, according to legend, are Aboriginal girls turned to stone by their father. He did so to protect them from a monster, but could not change them back again.

Beauchamp Falls, reached by the Grand Canyon Walk in the Blue Mountains.

Wentworth Falls. On these cliffs grows a rare dwarf conifer, a survivor from the distant past.

Above: Blue Gum forest in the Grose Valley.

Above: On the Grand Canyon Walking Track.

Walking on the wild side

A great way to enjoy all the Blue Mountains have to offer is by walking, and the National Parks and Wildlife Service of New South Wales maintains a number of trails which allow access to popular beauty spots. Less energetically obtained, but just as satisfying, are the views to be appreciated from the Scenic Skyway and Scenic Railway.

Opposite: A quiet moment in the Blue Mountains wilderness.

The Scenic Skyway carries passengers for 450 metres between two cliffs, on a cable nearly 300 metres above the Jamison Valley.

The Sceniscender is a cable car that drops 545 metres down the cliffs from Katoomba, below the rainforest canopy, into the Jamison Valley.

The world's steepest Scenic Railway descends 250 metres to the floor of the Jamison Valley.

Gardens of the Blue Mountains

Above: Mt Tomah Botanic Garden is owned by the Royal Botanic Gardens, Sydney.

The climate of the Blue Mountains is cooler than that of the coastal plains and over the years many beautiful gardens of exotic flowering plants, and some of native species, have been laid out around hotels, cottages and mansions. Katoomba, Leura, Blackheath and Springwood have particularly enchanting displays open to the public. There are many garden festivals held during the year, and the month of October alone offers the Wentworth Falls Spring Festival, the Leura Gardens Spring Festival, the Blue Mountains Herb Festival and the Blackheath Rhododendron Festival.

Opposite: Cool climate trees abound in Blue Mountains gardens.
Following pages: The Bacchante Gardens, site of the Blackheath Rhododendron Festival.

The Zig-Zag Railway was constructed between 1866 and 1869 over stone viaducts and through cuttings. Abandoned in 1910, it has been restored by railway enthusiasts.

The Jenolan Caves (there are at least 300) were formed when the Jenolan River dissolved minerals in the limestone of the Jenolan Valley.

Over the ranges

Above: The Nandewar Range from the summit of Mt Kaputar, Mt Kaputar National Park.

Once the traveller has passed over the Great Divide, there are a number of rugged ranges which rise into the bright blue inland skies. The Moonbi Range is near Tamworth, Country Music Capital of Australia, in fertile farmland. North-west of Tamworth is Mt Kaputar, with its own national park, a place of dramatic wild landscapes carved from an ancient volcano by 17 million years of erosion.

Opposite: Moonbi Pass, where the New England Highway runs through the Moonbi Range between Tamworth and Armidale.
Following pages: Pastoral scene near Gunnedah, west of Tamworth.

Warrumbungle National Park

The memorable wilderness of Warrumbungle National Park lies 33 kilometres west of Coonabarabran and about 500 kilometres north-west of Sydney. The park is ideal for walkers, climbers, campers and nature lovers, with a network of trails providing access to some spectacular natural features.

The park's rugged landscapes are volcanic in origin: millions of years of weathering have laid bare old lava flows and the plugs of cooled, solidified lava which once filled the necks of craters. In this grand setting, the plants and animals of the moist east coastal fringe of Australia meet those of the hotter, drier scrublands of the inland deserts.

The Breadknife, a famous feature of Warrumbungle National Park, was formed when lava forced its way into a narrow crack in the rock, solidified there and was later exposed by weathering away of surrounding layers.

Mungo National Park

Lunette dunes at Lake Mungo. Once, long ago, this area was rich in plant and animal life and occupied by groups of Aboriginal people.

Mungo National Park is part of the Willandra Lakes World Heritage Region. The lakes existed in an era when Australia was far wetter and rivers formed a chain of waterways in the area which is now south-western New South Wales. Today, wind has moved sand and clay from long-dry lake beds to form lunette dunes, in which lie fossils showing Aboriginal occupation of the area up to 35 000 or more years ago.

The Darling River

The Darling River in Kinchega National Park, near Menindee, western New South Wales.

A map of the central west of New South Wales shows many lakes and a number of rivers. In reality, most of these are dry, and many are salt-covered, springing to life only after substantial rain has fallen. The Darling River flows slowly from the north-east of the State to the far south-west, for much of its lower course providing green oases along its banks.

Above: Broken Hill's Argent Street, with the city's Post Office and Town Hall.

Above: The Trades Hall, built in 1905, is a solid stone building.

Broken Hill

In the far west of New South Wales, the mining city of Broken Hill is an oasis of green gardens and pleasant shady homes. An enormous lode of silver was discovered here in the early 1880s, in ore which also yields lead and zinc. By the early years of the twentieth century, the ore and wool which had been carried from the area in riverboats plying the Darling was being carried by rail and later by road.

Today, Broken Hill is a thriving modern city, relying on its mines and the surrounding pastoral leases for income, but with a soul refreshed by frequent doses of culture. This desert city has more art galleries and artists that most larger centres, a major Entertainment Complex and a thriving career as a location for Australian-made films.

Opposite: Hotel in Silverton, a mining "ghost town" near Broken Hill which is now a home for artists and a film location.

114

Exploring New South Wales

New South Wales is known to many as the Premier State, and certainly contains many prime attractions for the adventurer. It is easy to become fascinated by Sydney, a great city, distinctively Australian in style, and with its own unique signature of so many outstanding features: Sydney Harbour and its famous Bridge, Opera House, Darling Harbour and so on. However, after savouring the sophistication of the State capital, why not take the highway north to one of the world's great holiday coasts, or test the scenic appeal and holiday potential of the seaside south of Wollongong? Go west to the Blue Mountains, cross them and discover the wide plains of the Outback, take a right hand turn to the Warrumbungles or a left to the Murray River...

There is so much to see and do in this wonderful State, with its wide range of climates and variety of scenic delights. New South Wales is rich in culture, history, wildlife, and natural wonders. Every road leads to a new discovery.

Enjoy your adventures in this great State of New South Wales.

Steve Parish

World-famous photographer Steve Parish began his remarkable career by recording marine life off Australia's coasts. After discovering the fascinations of the rainforest and the wild creatures within it, he spent much of his time journeying around Australia photographing the landscapes, plants, animals and people of the land, and then extended the range of his subjects to include Australia's cities and towns.

The magnificent library of images that has resulted has become the heart of Steve Parish Publishing Pty Ltd. Through the firm's publications, Steve is realising his dream of sharing Australia with the world.

Celebrating Australia is a collection that presents the incomparable beauty of the southern continent in superb photographs and text. As Steve comments: "After a lifetime of travel and asking questions, I have only just begun to discover how much there is to learn about Australia. I hope these books arouse in others a desire like mine to explore and to appreciate this wonderful country."

Index

First published by Steve Parish Publishing Pty Ltd
PO Box 1058, Archerfield, Queensland 4108 Australia
© copyright Steve Parish Publishing Pty Ltd
www.steveparish.com.au
ISBN 174021078 6
Photography: Steve Parish
Text: Pat Slater, SPP

All rights reserved. No part of this publication may be reproduced, stored in a retrieval system, or transmitted in any form or by any means, electronic, mechanical, photocopying, recording or otherwise, without the prior permission in writing of the Publisher.

Photographic assistance by Phillip Hayson (front cover, pp 4–5, 6–7, 8–9, 12–13, 14–15, 20–21)
Additional photos supplied by The Photo Library (Allan Hedges, p 103)
Map supplied by MAPgraphics, Brisbane, Australia
Printed in Singapore by Nippecraft Limited
Produced at the Steve Parish Publishing Studios, Australia